Incident Report Book
Documentation! Documentation! Documentation!

This book is a vital tool for documenting and tracking important incidents, behaviors, and progress related to your students, clients, or patients. By keeping accurate and detailed records, you can support effective interventions, monitor growth, and ensure proper communication with colleagues and guardians. Use this book to enhance your ability to provide care, guidance, and support in a professional and accountable manner.

To get started, here are a few instructions to keep in mind:

1. **Record incidents promptly.** It is important to record incidents in the Incident Report Book as soon as possible after they occur. This helps ensure that details are fresh in your mind and that the incident is accurately recorded.
2. **Provide as much detail as possible.** This will include the date, time, location, individuals involved, and a description of what happened. The more detail you provide, the more useful the report will be in the future.
3. **Be objective.** When recording an incident, strive to be objective and avoid including personal opinions or biases. Stick to the facts of what happened and save your emotions for the final question, "How did this incident make you feel?"
4. **Use clear, concise and legible language.** This makes it easier for others to read and understand the report.
5. **Keep the Incident Report Book in a safe and secure place.** This helps protect the privacy of individuals involved in incidents, as well as yourself, and ensures that the reports are not tampered with.

The author has provided the information in this book as a service to the general public. The author is not a lawyer. Anyone seeking specific legal advice or assistance should retain an attorney. The author is not liable for how this book is used in any way.

Incident Type: ____

Date: _______________ Time: _________________

Location: ____

Specific area of location: _____________________________

All person(s) involved: ________________________________

____

____

Any witnesses' names: _________________________________

____

Incident description in detail (including any events leading up to or immediately following the incident): ______________________

____

____

____

____

____

____

____

____

____

____

____

____

____

____

____

____

____

____

____

____

____

____

____

____

____

Treatment/follow-up/prevention actions: _______________________________

____

____

How did this incident make you feel? _______________________________

____

Incident Type: ____

Date: _______________ Time: _________________

Location: ____

Specific area of location: _______________________________

All person(s) involved: __________________________________

____

____

Any witnesses' names: ____________________________________

____

Incident description in detail (including any events leading up to or immediately following the incident): ______________________

____

____

____

____

____

____

____

____

____

____

____

____

Treatment/follow-up/prevention actions: _______________________________

____

____

How did this incident make you feel? ___________________________________

____

Incident Type: ____

Date: _______________ Time: _______________________

Location: ____

Specific area of location: ____

All person(s) involved: ____

____

____

Any witnesses' names: ____

____

Incident description in detail (including any events leading up to or
immediately following the incident): ______________________________________

____

____

____

____

____

____

____

____

____

____

____

____

____

____

____

____

____

____

____

____

____

____

____

____

____

____

Treatment/follow-up/prevention actions: ______________________

____

____

How did this incident make you feel? ______________________

____

Incident Type: ____

Date: _______________ Time: _________________

Location: ____

Specific area of location: _________________________________

All person(s) involved: ____________________________________

____

____

Any witnesses' names: _____________________________________

____

Incident description in detail (including any events leading up to or immediately following the incident): _____________________________

____

____

____

____

____

____

____

____

____

____

____

____

____

____

____

____

____

____

____

____

____

____

____

____

Treatment/follow-up/prevention actions: _______________________________

____

____

How did this incident make you feel? _______________________________

____

Incident Type: ____

Date: _______________ Time: _________________

Location: ____

Specific area of location: ____

All person(s) involved: ____

____

____

Any witnesses' names: ____

____

Incident description in detail (including any events leading up to or immediately following the incident): ______________________________________

____

____

____

____

____

____

____

____

____

____

____

____

____

____

____

____

____

____

____

____

____

____

Treatment/follow-up/prevention actions: _______________________

____

____

How did this incident make you feel? ________________________

____

Incident Type: ____

Date: ________________ Time: ________________

Location: ____

Specific area of location: ____________________________

All person(s) involved: _______________________________

____

____

Any witnesses' names: _________________________________

____

Incident description in detail (including any events leading up to or immediately following the incident): _______________________

____

____

____

____

____

____

____

____

____

____

____

____

____

____

____

____

____

____

____

____

____

____

____

Treatment/follow-up/prevention actions: __________________

____

____

How did this incident make you feel? ____________________

____

Incident Type: ____

Date: ________________ Time: __________________

Location: ____

Specific area of location: ____

All person(s) involved: ____

____

____

Any witnesses' names: ____

____

Incident description in detail (including any events leading up to or immediately following the incident): ___________________________________

____

____

____

____

____

____

____

____

____

____

____

____

____

____

____

____

____

____

____

____

____

____

____

____

____

Treatment/follow-up/prevention actions: _______________________________

____

____

How did this incident make you feel? _______________________________

____

Incident Type: ____

Date: _______________ Time: __________________

Location: ____

Specific area of location: ____

All person(s) involved: ____

____

____

Any witnesses' names: ____

____

Incident description in detail (including any events leading up to or
immediately following the incident): ____________________________________

____

____

____

____

____

____

____

____

____

____

____

Treatment/follow-up/prevention actions: _______________________________

____

____

How did this incident make you feel? _______________________________

____

Incident Type: ____

Date: ________________ Time: _________________

Location: ____

Specific area of location: ____________________________________

All person(s) involved: _______________________________________

____

____

Any witnesses' names: ____

____

Incident description in detail (including any events leading up to or immediately following the incident): ___________________________

____

____

____

____

____

____

____

____

____

____

____

Treatment/follow-up/prevention actions: _______________________

____

How did this incident make you feel? _______________________

Incident Type: ____

Date: _______________ Time: _________________

Location: ____

Specific area of location: _____________________________________

All person(s) involved: ____

____

____

Any witnesses' names: ____

____

Incident description in detail (including any events leading up to or immediately following the incident): _______________________

____

____

____

____

____

____

____

____

____

____

____

____

____

____

____

____

____

____

____

____

____

____

____

____

____

Treatment/follow-up/prevention actions: _______________________

____

____

How did this incident make you feel? _______________________

____

Incident Type: ____

Date: _______________ Time: _________________

Location: ____

Specific area of location: ____

All person(s) involved: ____

____

____

Any witnesses' names: ____

____

Incident description in detail (including any events leading up to or

immediately following the incident): _________________________________

____

____

____

____

____

____

____

____

____

____

____

____

____

____

____

____

____

____

____

____

____

____

____

____

Treatment/follow-up/prevention actions: ______________________

____

____

How did this incident make you feel? ______________________

____

Incident Type: ____

Date: ______________ Time: ___________________

Location: ____

Specific area of location: ______________________________

All person(s) involved: _________________________________

____

____

Any witnesses' names: _________________________________

____

Incident description in detail (including any events leading up to or immediately following the incident): _______________________

____

____

____

____

____

____

____

____

____

____

____

Treatment/follow-up/prevention actions: _______________________________

____

____

How did this incident make you feel? ___________________________________

____

Incident Type: ____

Date: _______________ Time: _______________________

Location: ____

Specific area of location: _____________________________________

All person(s) involved: ____

____

____

Any witnesses' names: ____

____

Incident description in detail (including any events leading up to or
immediately following the incident): _____________________________

____

____

____

____

____

____

____

____

____

____

____

____

____

____

____

____

____

____

____

____

____

____

____

____

____

Treatment/follow-up/prevention actions: _______________________

____

____

How did this incident make you feel? _______________________

____

Incident Type: ____

Date: _______________ Time: _______________

Location: ____

Specific area of location: ____________________________________

All person(s) involved: _______________________________________

____

____

Any witnesses' names: ____

____

Incident description in detail (including any events leading up to or immediately following the incident): _______________________

____

____

____

____

____

____

____

____

____

____

____

____

____

____

____

____

____

____

____

____

____

____

____

____

____

____

____

Treatment/follow-up/prevention actions: ________________________________

____

____

How did this incident make you feel? ________________________________

____

Incident Type: ____

Date: ______________ Time: ________________

Location: ____

Specific area of location: ______________________________________

All person(s) involved: ____

____

____

Any witnesses' names: ____

____

Incident description in detail (including any events leading up to or
immediately following the incident): _______________________________

____

____

____

____

____

____

____

____

____

____

____

____

____

____

____

____

____

____

____

____

____

____

____

____

____

Treatment/follow-up/prevention actions: _______________________

____

____

How did this incident make you feel? _______________________

____

Incident Type: ____

Date: _______________ Time: _______________

Location: ____

Specific area of location: _____________________________________

All person(s) involved: ____

____

____

Any witnesses' names: ____

____

Incident description in detail (including any events leading up to or immediately following the incident): _________________________________

____

____

____

____

____

____

____

____

____

____

____

Treatment/follow-up/prevention actions: _______________________________

____

____

How did this incident make you feel? _______________________________

____

Incident Type: ____

Date: _______________ Time: _________________

Location: ____

Specific area of location: ____

All person(s) involved: ____

____

____

Any witnesses' names: ____

____

Incident description in detail (including any events leading up to or immediately following the incident): ________________________________

____

____

____

____

____

____

____

____

____

____

____

____

____

____

____

____

____

____

____

____

____

____

____

____

____

Treatment/follow-up/prevention actions: _______________________

____

____

How did this incident make you feel? _______________________

____

Incident Type: ____

Date: ______________ Time: ________________

Location: ____

Specific area of location: ___________________________________

All person(s) involved: ______________________________________

____

____

Any witnesses' names: ____

____

Incident description in detail (including any events leading up to or immediately following the incident): _______________________

____

____

____

____

____

____

____

____

____

____

____

Treatment/follow-up/prevention actions: _______________________________

How did this incident make you feel? _______________________________

Incident Type: ____

Date: _______________ Time: _______________

Location: ____

Specific area of location: _______________________________

All person(s) involved: _________________________________

____

____

Any witnesses' names: __________________________________

____

Incident description in detail (including any events leading up to or immediately following the incident): _______________________

____

____

____

____

____

____

____

____

____

____

____

Treatment/follow-up/prevention actions: _______________________________

How did this incident make you feel? _______________________________

Incident Type: ____

Date: _______________ Time: _________________

Location: ____

Specific area of location: ____________________________________

All person(s) involved: _______________________________________

____

____

Any witnesses' names: ____

____

Incident description in detail (including any events leading up to or
immediately following the incident): __________________________

____

____

____

____

____

____

____

____

____

____

____

____

____

____

____

____

____

____

____

____

____

____

____

____

Treatment/follow-up/prevention actions: _______________________

____

____

How did this incident make you feel? _______________________

____

Incident Type: ____

Date: _______________ Time: ___________________

Location: ____

Specific area of location: ____________________________________

All person(s) involved: _______________________________________

____

____

Any witnesses' names: _______________________________________

____

Incident description in detail (including any events leading up to or immediately following the incident): ___________________________

____

____

____

____

____

____

____

____

____

____

____

____

____

____

____

____

____

____

____

____

____

____

____

____

Treatment/follow-up/prevention actions: ______________________________

____

____

How did this incident make you feel? _______________________________

____

Incident Type: ____

Date: _______________ Time: _________________

Location: ____

Specific area of location: ____________________________________

All person(s) involved: _______________________________________

____

____

Any witnesses' names: ____

____

Incident description in detail (including any events leading up to or immediately following the incident): _______________________________

____

____

____

____

____

____

____

____

____

____

____

Treatment/follow-up/prevention actions: ___________________________

____

____

How did this incident make you feel? ______________________________

____

Incident Type: ____

Date: _______________ Time: _________________

Location: ____

Specific area of location: _______________________________

All person(s) involved: _________________________________

____

____

Any witnesses' names: _________________________________

____

Incident description in detail (including any events leading up to or immediately following the incident): ______________________________

____

____

____

____

____

____

____

____

____

____

____

Treatment/follow-up/prevention actions: _______________________

____

____

How did this incident make you feel? _______________________

____

Incident Type: ____

Date: ________________ Time: ____________________

Location: ____

Specific area of location: ___________________________________

All person(s) involved: ______________________________________

____

____

Any witnesses' names: ____

____

Incident description in detail (including any events leading up to or immediately following the incident): _______________________

____

____

____

____

____

____

____

____

____

____

____

____

Treatment/follow-up/prevention actions: _______________________

How did this incident make you feel? _______________________

Incident Type: ____

Date: ______________ Time: ________________

Location: ____

Specific area of location: ____________________________________

All person(s) involved: _______________________________________

____

____

Any witnesses' names: _______________________________________

____

Incident description in detail (including any events leading up to or
immediately following the incident): ___________________________

____

____

____

____

____

____

____

____

____

____

____

Treatment/follow-up/prevention actions: ______________________________

____

____

How did this incident make you feel? ______________________________

____

Incident Type: ____

Date: _______________ Time: _________________

Location: ____

Specific area of location: ____________________________________

All person(s) involved: _______________________________________

____

____

Any witnesses' names: ____

____

Incident description in detail (including any events leading up to or
immediately following the incident): ___________________________

____

____

____

____

____

____

____

____

____

____

____

Treatment/follow-up/prevention actions: _______________________

____

____

How did this incident make you feel? ___________________________

____

Incident Type: ____

Date: _______________ Time: ________________

Location: ____

Specific area of location: ______________________________

All person(s) involved: _________________________________

____

____

Any witnesses' names: __________________________________

____

Incident description in detail (including any events leading up to or immediately following the incident): ________________________

____

____

____

____

____

____

____

____

____

____

____

____

Treatment/follow-up/prevention actions: _______________________________

____

____

____

How did this incident make you feel? ___________________________________

____

Incident Type: ____

Date: _______________ Time: _________________

Location: ____

Specific area of location: ________________________________

All person(s) involved: ___________________________________

____

____

Any witnesses' names: _____________________________________

____

Incident description in detail (including any events leading up to or immediately following the incident): _______________________

____

____

____

____

____

____

____

____

____

____

____

Treatment/follow-up/prevention actions: _______________________________

____

How did this incident make you feel? ___________________________________

____

Incident Type: ____

Date: _______________ Time: _________________

Location: ____

Specific area of location: ____________________________________

All person(s) involved: _______________________________________

____

____

Any witnesses' names: ____

____

Incident description in detail (including any events leading up to or immediately following the incident): ____________________________

____

____

____

____

____

____

____

____

____

____

____

Treatment/follow-up/prevention actions: _______________________

____

____

How did this incident make you feel? ___________________________

____

Incident Type: ____

Date: _______________ Time: _________________

Location: ____

Specific area of location: ____________________________________

All person(s) involved: _______________________________________

____

____

Any witnesses' names: ____

____

Incident description in detail (including any events leading up to or
immediately following the incident): __________________________

____

____

____

____

____

____

____

____

____

____

____

Treatment/follow-up/prevention actions: _______________________________

____

____

How did this incident make you feel? _______________________________

____

Incident Type: ____

Date: _______________ Time: ________________

Location: ____

Specific area of location: ____________________________________

All person(s) involved: _______________________________________

____

____

Any witnesses' names: ____

____

Incident description in detail (including any events leading up to or

immediately following the incident): __________________________

____

____

____

____

____

____

____

____

____

____

____

Treatment/follow-up/prevention actions: _______________________

____

____

How did this incident make you feel? ___________________________

____

Incident Type: ____

Date: _______________ Time: _______________

Location: ____

Specific area of location: ____

All person(s) involved: ____

____

____

Any witnesses' names: ____

____

Incident description in detail (including any events leading up to or immediately following the incident): ____

____

____

____

____

____

____

____

____

____

____

____

Treatment/follow-up/prevention actions: _______________________

____

____

____

How did this incident make you feel? _________________________

____

Incident Type: ____

Date: _______________ Time: _________________

Location: ____

Specific area of location: ___________________________________

All person(s) involved: ______________________________________

____

____

Any witnesses' names: ____

____

Incident description in detail (including any events leading up to or
immediately following the incident): ________________________

____

____

____

____

____

____

____

____

____

____

____

Treatment/follow-up/prevention actions: ___________________________

____

____

How did this incident make you feel? ___________________________

____

Incident Type: ____

Date: ________________ Time: __________________

Location: ____

Specific area of location: ______________________________

All person(s) involved: ________________________________

____

____

Any witnesses' names: ________________________________

____

Incident description in detail (including any events leading up to or
immediately following the incident): _______________________

____

____

____

____

____

____

____

____

____

____

____

Treatment/follow-up/prevention actions: ___________________________

How did this incident make you feel? ___________________________

Incident Type: ____

Date: ______________ Time: ________________

Location: ____

Specific area of location: ______________________________________

All person(s) involved: ____

____

____

Any witnesses' names: ____

____

Incident description in detail (including any events leading up to or immediately following the incident): ______________________________

____

____

____

____

____

____

____

____

____

____

____

Treatment/follow-up/prevention actions: _______________________________

How did this incident make you feel? _______________________________

Incident Type: ____

Date: _______________ Time: _________________

Location: ____

Specific area of location: _______________________________________

All person(s) involved: ____

____

____

Any witnesses' names: ____

____

Incident description in detail (including any events leading up to or
immediately following the incident): ____________________________

____

____

____

____

____

____

____

____

____

____

____

____

____

____

____

____

____

____

____

____

____

____

____

____

____

Treatment/follow-up/prevention actions: ___________________________

____

____

How did this incident make you feel? ___________________________

____

Incident Type: ____

Date: _______________ Time: _________________

Location: ____

Specific area of location: _____________________________________

All person(s) involved: ____

____

____

Any witnesses' names: ____

____

Incident description in detail (including any events leading up to or immediately following the incident): _______________________________

____

____

____

____

____

____

____

____

____

____

____

____

Treatment/follow-up/prevention actions: _______________________

How did this incident make you feel? _______________________

Incident Type: ____

Date: _______________ Time: _________________

Location: ____

Specific area of location: ______________________________

All person(s) involved: _________________________________

____

____

Any witnesses' names: _________________________________

____

Incident description in detail (including any events leading up to or immediately following the incident): _______________________

____

____

____

____

____

____

____

____

____

____

____

Treatment/follow-up/prevention actions: _______________________

How did this incident make you feel? _______________________

Incident Type: ____

Date: ________________ Time: __________________

Location: ____

Specific area of location: _____________________________________

All person(s) involved: ____

____

____

Any witnesses' names: ____

____

Incident description in detail (including any events leading up to or

immediately following the incident): _____________________________

____

____

____

____

____

____

____

____

____

____

____

____

____

____

____

____

____

____

____

____

____

____

____

____

____

____

Treatment/follow-up/prevention actions: _______________________

____

____

How did this incident make you feel? _______________________

____

Incident Type: ____

Date: ______________ Time: ________________

Location: ____

Specific area of location: ____________________________________

All person(s) involved: _______________________________________

____

____

Any witnesses' names: ____

____

Incident description in detail (including any events leading up to or
immediately following the incident): __________________________

____

____

____

____

____

____

____

____

____

____

____

Treatment/follow-up/prevention actions: _______________________________

How did this incident make you feel? _______________________________

Incident Type: ____

Date: _______________ Time: _______________

Location: ____

Specific area of location: ______________________________

All person(s) involved: _________________________________

____

____

Any witnesses' names: __________________________________

____

Incident description in detail (including any events leading up to or immediately following the incident): __________________________

____

____

____

____

____

____

____

____

____

____

____

Treatment/follow-up/prevention actions: _______________________

How did this incident make you feel? _______________________

Incident Type: ____

Date: ______________ Time: ____________________

Location: ____

Specific area of location: ____________________________

All person(s) involved: _______________________________

____

____

Any witnesses' names: _________________________________

____

Incident description in detail (including any events leading up to or
immediately following the incident): __________________________

____

____

____

____

____

____

____

____

____

____

____

Treatment/follow-up/prevention actions: _______________________________

How did this incident make you feel? _______________________________

Incident Type: ____

Date: _______________ Time: _________________

Location: ____

Specific area of location: _______________________________

All person(s) involved: _________________________________

____

____

Any witnesses' names: __________________________________

____

Incident description in detail (including any events leading up to or immediately following the incident): ________________________

____

____

____

____

____

____

____

____

____

____

____

____

____

____

____

____

____

____

____

____

____

____

____

____

____

____

Treatment/follow-up/prevention actions: _______________________

____

____

How did this incident make you feel? _______________________

____

Incident Type: ____

Date: _______________ Time: _________________

Location: ____

Specific area of location: _______________________________

All person(s) involved: __________________________________

____

____

Any witnesses' names: __________________________________

____

Incident description in detail (including any events leading up to or immediately following the incident): ___________________________

____

____

____

____

____

____

____

____

____

____

____

____

____

____

____

____

____

____

____

____

____

____

____

____

____

Treatment/follow-up/prevention actions: _______________

____

____

How did this incident make you feel? _______________

____

Incident Type: ____

Date: _______________ Time: _________________

Location: ____

Specific area of location: _________________________________

All person(s) involved: ____________________________________

____

____

Any witnesses' names: ____________________________________

____

Incident description in detail (including any events leading up to or
immediately following the incident): ________________________

____

____

____

____

____

____

____

____

____

____

____

Treatment/follow-up/prevention actions: ___________________________________

How did this incident make you feel? ___________________________________

Incident Type: ____

Date: ______________ Time: __________________

Location: ____

Specific area of location: ________________________________

All person(s) involved: ___________________________________

____

____

Any witnesses' names: ____________________________________

____

Incident description in detail (including any events leading up to or
immediately following the incident): _______________________

____

____

____

____

____

____

____

____

____

____

____

Treatment/follow-up/prevention actions: _______________________________

____

How did this incident make you feel? ________________________________

Incident Type: ____

Date: _______________ Time: ___________________

Location: ____

Specific area of location: _________________________________

All person(s) involved: ___________________________________

____

____

Any witnesses' names: ____________________________________

____

Incident description in detail (including any events leading up to or immediately following the incident): ______________________

____

____

____

____

____

____

____

____

____

____

____

Treatment/follow-up/prevention actions: ______________________

How did this incident make you feel? ______________________

Incident Type: ____

Date: _______________ Time: _______________

Location: ____

Specific area of location: ____________________________________

All person(s) involved: _______________________________________

____

____

Any witnesses' names: ____

____

Incident description in detail (including any events leading up to or immediately following the incident): _______________________

____

____

____

____

____

____

____

____

____

____

____

____

____

____

____

____

____

____

____

____

____

____

____

____

Treatment/follow-up/prevention actions: _______________________

____

____

How did this incident make you feel? _______________________

____

Gratitude

Thank you for using this Incident Report Book. We understand that working with students, clients, and families can be both rewarding and challenging. Whether you're addressing behavioral concerns, tracking progress, or documenting critical incidents, your work is invaluable in providing the care, guidance, and support that others depend on.

Your commitment to maintaining accurate records is essential in ensuring that those in your care receive the best possible interventions, support, and attention. By documenting incidents and progress, you're creating a foundation for positive change and accountability.

We hope that this Incident Report Book has empowered you in your professional journey, helping you continue your vital work with clarity, compassion, and confidence.

If this book has helped you, we'd love to hear about it. Please send your story to stories@oursteadyprogress.com.

Take care and stay strong. Welcome to the revolution for a more equitable future.

~ Our Steady Progress

Printed in Great Britain
by Amazon

48526586R00057